4 Greek Women
Love Poems

translated by
Eleni Fourtouni

Eleni Fourtouni

THELPHINI PRESS

Copyright © 1982 by *Thelphini Press*

The translation of this book was funded by a grant from the National Endowment for the Arts.

No portion of this book may be reproduced without the written permission of the publisher, except by reviewers writing for the public press. Address inquiries to Thelphini Press, 1218 Forest Road, New Haven, Connecticut.

This book was printed in Athens by «ΘΥΜΕΛΗ», τηλ. 3607.822

For all the Aegean Women

Contents

VICTORIA THEODOROU   9

ANGELIKI PAVLOPOULOU   33

KATERINA ANGHELAKI-ROOKE   47

ELENI FOURTOUNI   61

Victoria Theodorou

Victoria Theodorou was born in 1928 in Crete of a Cretan mother and Yugoslavian father. She studied literature at the University of Athens. During the Second World War she participated in the resistance movement against the Germans. For this she was imprisoned by the right wing government which ruled Greece after the war, together with thousands of other men and women also members of that resistance, in various island concentration camps for five years.

Theodorou lives in Athens with her husband and two daughters. She's the author of several books of poetry and prose. During her exile she wrote a journal — a moving account about the life and the type of organization the women had in the camps. Her journal and that of another exiled woman will be published in English translation this fall.

Her work has been translated into French, Yugoslavian, and Rumanian. English versions of her work are included in *Greek Women Poets*.

From THE LUTE

1.

Where are you going in this sleet, this blizzard,
this cold will freeze your heart as it would a starling.
Where are you running,
fearless in these windy streets,
slender as you are and tiny,
—I'm going to give this body up to love,
this bitter mouth to kisses.
Now I must do it, before my fate turns
and shrivels it with fever and disease,
for they've insulted and beaten it,
starved and kept it from the sun.
An offering to love's sweet pleasure
I'll make of it,
for they've confined it and drained it without asking its will, its limit
It is my body, and mine is its pain
its sickness and its death—
and when the hour comes, alone I will die—
but today I will it in my lover's arms,
on that river of my song to glide.

2.

Fragrance, gladness of my life, my untimely
unwise love
my chapel and beehive
fruitful apple tree—beneath your shade
I lie
with eager wise hands—
refuge and unexpected cave
shelter from man-eating beasts
cave with wild doves
hung with stalactites
gentle deer, music of leaves and water
flute from green bamboo, wild berry
bittersweet, spicy mouth
my laurel and my mead
lute with the wild chords
for me alone is your music.

3.

Wings I have forged for you,
a wind-driven ship to lift you up
from your citadel to take you
from your lords to free you.

Love, I say, is fire is air
nothing can stand its might
But you are heavy-set bulky and hard.

4.

Forgive me if I don't hear,
don't take in the meaning of your words
I'm dazed by the play of your coral lips,
the luster of your teeth blinds me,
and the wild lute chords of your speech
make me drunk.

5.

How lovely, how young you are
in my arms, how you smell!
You are a shrub after the rain—
vivid colors, fragrant vapors,
and your smile like sandalwood.

If I am the cloud spraying you,
the breeze giving you life,
there's my renown,
there's my jewels and riches.

6.

Neither fierce winds nor gentle breezes
brimming with balm and fragrance
have ever torn a single scarf off my head.
Their might breaks against my stubbornness
against my fragile frame.
West and east winds
like dying birds expire, as do
the other two—most powerful—
so convinced of their ardor.

But your splendid eyes
with love alone
caused my robes to fall.

Music I found dormant in my heart
and I swayed and danced
beneath the sun of your gaze.

7.

Come now,
not when I'm sick and old.
In my youth, in my prime come.
When my hands brim over
and I know not how to unburden
my heart of all this gladness.

Now, when I choke with sap, and bend
like a slender tree, burdened with much fruit.

Later, go away. Alone I want to take
the road of my decay.
Your pity, whether true or false,
I will never need.

8.

I come to this island,
this out-of-the-way harbor,
myself, water, seaweed,
a single sand-pine on the beach.
Scorched, parched, I plunge
and plunge again, I emerge refreshed,
forged in metal. I create myself
without memory. The salt, the sun——my scars
and ointments, my only hurt the sea-urchin's needle.
Healed, I sleep on this forgotten shore——a scrap
of wood thrown out of a shipyard,
without need of flax and tar
for my many cracks,
I plan no voyage, no return.
I exist and I don't exist,
as before I was born,
as when I die.
I practice solitude, I learn loneliness
by this cliff that challenges the ocean.

I come to this island
this out-of the-way harbor,
but the ship with the many masts
will find me, I know,
and without asking it will bring me back
the city streets to roam
again——searching for the green diamond,
for the white camel.

9.

How that "nay" crushes me
each nightfall, how it wounds me.
And yet, my lips only spoke it,
the mouth willed it on its own.
My heart protests
and scolds me now——who decides,
who is the master here——the heart asks,
demands to know.
That "nay" grows immense each nightfall,
it screeches like a blue jay in the trees.

Pay for your pride now
hug your virtue that will not warm you,
get through the blizzard on your own,
eat with that "nay" next to you,
take it in your arms when you lie down.

10.

No, these aren't curtains on my window,
It's ivy wound around
the barren almond tree.

Like ivy you feed off my sap,
and I'll never bear another fruit.
I used to flower once
and planned to seed a forest,
but you nailed me down with your needy roots—
parasitic vine, you cling on my trunk.

From your clasp
nothing can ever save me,
nothing but the woodcutter's ax.

11.

Pressed between the pages of a book——
cyclamens——their exquisite lines,
their delicate, lacelike border——intact.
Dry wildflowers in a crystal vase, seeds——
enough to make a valley bloom——inside the calyx.

If he loves them——these flowers long past
their prime, lacking all moisture and color——
perhaps my face too can hold his loving gaze.

*From URANIA**

1.

A universe of fury and mystery
has engendered you, *Espere***.
But you have risen as a gentle star.
Your silver glance sustains me,
your orbit marks my bounds,
you are the necessary rhythm of my heart,
my soul's equilibrium.
When you sink beneath the rim of heaven
the wonder of your next ascent
you leave on my palm.
And you will not forsake me
until, transmuted into breeze,
I too will caress
the waters and the leaves.

You, who explore the roots
and the origins of the roots, have chosen me,
given me an undemanded pledge,
marked my door——a guest to my silence.

* *Another name for Aphrodite*
** *The evening star*

2.

I saw you rise over the vineyards—
in your lightbeams the vines
were enthralled.
I saw you over the sea
and the waves envied you,
from my cell's window I greeted you,
from the arms of love,
over the fires of war I saw you.

Master and slave to no man,
I desired and claimed you,
knowing you belong
to all eyes that see you.

3.

My footsteps you follow,
their lacelike prints minutely you examine,
you scrutinize my wonderings,
you judge, presume, misunderstand.
You will not find the key to my movements,
I'm not water that flows from spring to lake,
and there turns to vapor,
I'm more intricate than you can ever guess—
there's old age in my youth,
youth springs out of my old age,
night is day for me, dawn is dusk,
in my laughter there are tears that feed
seeds of gladness.

I'm of a time long past—so long
you think I come from tomorrow,
and I'm monotonous,
like an old Pondus lyre.

4.

I will wait
until the thick shadows of planets pass over,
until the orbit of his words
reaches my firmament——cruelly tried
and jeered by stampeding minions,
bulls and snake-bearing giants,
brutal hunters, dragons and bruins.
When he rises——immense and deliberate——
he will crush violence,
will silence evil tongues,
and he will know me,
the one I am, the one I will become,
the loyal, the peaceable,
the dispossessed of love.

5.

I cast duty off my leaves,
even the last fruit—intent on draining me
free in the wind, in the elements,
myself as element and as wind.
If *Urania* wants to grace me,
saps flow inside me still
if birds want to come,
I can hold them—
with their nests and their songs—
if I fall, I fall
forests will still grow around me,
seeds will scatter, will travel far.

6.

For him I've gained hearing,
sight to see him in the dark,
my heart——that dithyrambic
song——for him I've resurrected
in my burial grounds,
beneath the ancient bridge.

He called and promised
groves, gardens, fields,
larks and crystal springs.
Though in his ways ignorant, unschooled,
I heard the rage in his center, saw
the lava under his skin——
preparing earthquakes.

7.

I accept your call, but I warn you,
among earthly arbors I will walk once more.
Light's pure reflexion,
your golden glass aimed straight
in my eyes, blinds me.
Again I will dream
beneath silver poplar trees—
waiting to shelter me.
I come only for a while. You must know
that I will soon depart. Voices
and ineffable sounds
are calling me,
echoes knock on my door,
stirring my restless heart.

8.

Bedazzled with pageants of the sky,
I return
beneath the familiar breathing
of vine arbors.
Passion begotten by lightning
must die the same way.
The Goddess in her upper rooms,
the all powerful, wise *Urania*
(though she's but a figment of our
human imaginings) decreed it so.

I practice in loneliness now,
I learn to survive with empty hands,
like Arktouros who in vain trails
his bride, his passion
a bright torch——summer's harbinger, eternal.

9.

Bright fountain——between seasons of darkness,
laughter——between seasons of grief,
speech and song——between seasons of silence,
answer me:
why did you blaze, why did you ripple,
why did you sing—
only to vanish once more?
Teach me, *Urania,* continuity's alchemy,
teach me how to hold
what I have myself begotten.

You grow dark green lake,
splendor of my sight you are dimming,
green riverbank you wither and recede—
the nests of starlings you leave unsheltered.

10.

Unyielding planet,
immutable,
the face of your destiny
will never change.
And if I must think, must speak—
without pause—
to escape death and sleep,
I will not be an owl
on the cypress tree screeching
the same solitary tune,
a dry riverbank, a sick bed,
an ocean of the moon.
I am the one who named you,
described you so that you can exist,
the one keeping you alive with my constant eyes.

What will become of you when I'm gone,
what will you do up high,
what good is your brilliance without my sight,
who will hear your music
when I'm gone?

11.

How he creaked on his pedestal
and slipped off his axle,
the invincible, the sorcerer,
he who bedazzled the worlds,
the insatiable of the seven heavens—
so bold to seize his prey.

Where is the master of my right arm,
the devourer of my song and passion now?
the infidel,
he flowed like mercury, like smoke
in his arrogance dissolved, unravelled
like a cloud and he's gone.

Angeliki Pavlopoulou

Angeliki Pavlopoulou was born in 1930, in the historical town of Mesologgi, where during the 1821 Greek War of Independence. Lord Byron lived, wrote, and died during that struggle.
Angeliki still lives in Mesologgi where, to use her own words, she «cultivates her fields and poetry».

ANGELIKI PAVLOPOULOU

From EROTIC INSPECTIONS

1.

Boys of a full-blooded race
don't waste your youth walking alone
now when the earth is ready
and beneath every tree
lies the fabulous legend
of your first erotic chambers

full-blooded race
I welcome you

Women's Chorus

We
the first to emerge from these chambers
like bees
we'll gather your words
and the harvest will become sanctified—
an erotic song

2.

Look
there in the open fields
where the sun
always augments the harvest
the first cucumbers hang large
and the village boys
with the slender hips
fill their baskets
with the firm fruit
see how they gaze at the women
who bend down to take the harvest in

Women's Chorus

I'll tell you everything
bit by bit
but first
the way I see it
boys are like animals
they don't mix imagination
with sex

3.

Look
at these boys
when in the spring
they rush
in the cobbled streets
they're like slim-footed ewes
unburdened of their fleece

Women's Chorus

The delight and the torment of sex
when you taste it
thoroughly

Ah, daughters with the unbound breasts
in your domain
brimming with beeswax and light
there is time for dance

4.

And when the rain turns gentle
and there's shade under the trees
the boys gather in the forest
feasting with song
swallowing their sweet spittle
as the partridge swallows water
drop by drop by the riverbed

Women's Chorus

I say that you must not become enigmas
like the mute sea
when the boys chant
their lust

Ah, songs of resurrection

5.

Now
when the seedlings fill out
and green-over garden furrows
the ecstatic boys
try to touch
as high up as they can
above the calves of the women

Women's Chorus

From all God's blessings
sex, like the bell-crowned
ram leading the flocks,
will always lead us
on the right track

Ah, playful greetings
seductive night wanderings

6.

Everyone knows
why the doves murmur
under the rafters
like boys and girls
restless in their beds
for they still don't know
how to lie together

Women's Chorus

From my watchtower
I learn
one by one the signs
of the erotic code

Ah, the sign of unfulfillment

7.

Now is the season
when the earth crackles
with lust
the season when plants and trees shed
their useless blossoms
and struggle to form the fruit
and when girls
turn mellow
from that unbearable need for transformation

Women's Chorus

At times
the deities of the erotic
gather behind shrubs and bamboo thickets

Ah, virginal heirlooms
of those fleeting moments

8.

This is the season
when the eyes of the boys
become large
like autumn stars
as they unfasten the bodices
of their first girl
and draw their lips near
like moist leaves
turning
closer to the sun

Women's Chorus

It is now time to tell you
that the first revelation
happens when you see her
and then when you touch her

Ah, favorable omens
following the touch

9.

In the autumn
when the delicate leaves
can no longer hold onto the branches
the boys
possessed by ardor
behave clumsily
like butterflies and silkworms
who cannot locate
the secret parts of flowers

Women's Chorus

I proclaim
that we have inherited
this elemental lust
from the soil
and from the winged ones

Ah, sacred virgins
when you yield you flower

10.

In October
when we wait eagerly for the fields
to soak the rain in
stealthy deflowering
is in full swing

Women's Chorus

Times like these
fill me with the certainty
that everything
exists inside a mystical harmony and grace

Ah, blessed male wonder
traced in large script

11.

In midwinter
when strong winds
drive the rainstorms
slanted against houses
and you can't tell
earth from sky
the coffee shops are full of loiterers
who have never even glimpsed at God's face
but the young men
are driven by lust
and according to village gossip
they're often seen
in barns and stables
fondling the bosoms of girls

Women's Chorus

It is known that erotic ardor
mellows God's wrath

Ah, winter supplication
for appeasement

12.

Intimate hours
when in the fields
the wild chase begins
when the swallows fly
with open beaks
and the young girls
worn out from the cold
and that secret need
throw furtive looks at the bursting buds
of cherry trees
and wink
knowingly

Women's Chorus

Whatever happens
sex will always be sex
with sweet talk
and lewd signs

Ah, the ordained games of sex

Katerina Anghelaki-Rooke

Katerina Angelaki-Rooke was born in 1939, in Athens. Studied languages in Greece and Switzerland. Has visited America as a member of the Iowa International Writers Program, as a Ford Foundation fellow, and as a Fulbright professor at Harvard.
She is the author of six books of poetry, of many essays and criticism, and the translator of French, Russian, English, and American writers.
Katerina lives in a two hundred year old house on Aegina island where she writes, takes care of her pistachio orchard, and heals her friends' wounds with her laughter and love.
Other English translations of her work are included in *Greek Women Poets*.

From THE SCATTERED PAPERS OF PENELOPE

SAYS PENELOPE

I was not weaving or knitting
a story I was writing, rewriting
stifling
under the burden of words,
unable to reach perfection
with grief crushing my center.
Absence, always the subject of my life
—absence from life—
tears spring from the paper
and the natural anguish
of a deprived body.

Rewriting, tearing
stifling my living cries
Where are you, come, I'm waiting
this spring is not like others
and every morning I begin all over
with new birds and white linen
drying in the sun.
You will never be here
with the hose to water the flowers
the old ceiling dripping
soaked with rain,
and I, dissolving inside you
quietly, autumnlike...
Your exquisite heart
—exquisite because I've chosen it—
will always be elsewhere
and with words I will break
the threads binding me
to that certain man
for whom I long
until Odysseus becomes a symbol of longing

sailing the seas
of our brain.

I forget you with passion
every day
until washed from sweet smelling sin
and entirely clean at last
you'll enter immortality.
A hard and thankless task,
my only reward if finally I can understand
the meaning of existence
of absence
how the self can go on
in all that loneliness, endlessly,
how the body always rénews itself
it falls and it rises
as if axed down
afflicted or in love,
hoping
to gain the essence
of that which it can no longer touch.

TO THE EARTH

I speak to the earth today and I say:
Good earth with the night birds
silent and black winged
with chattering morning birds
with waters, salty and sweet—
they go their own way
bubbling, fondling
and of course indifferent.
Earth, you're all I know of the world
—even the sky's part of you
and you will cover me
like a soft blanket one day.

Talk to me, teach me, tell me
that we must not mourn the living
even if we thirst for them
like the dry tongue thirsts for water,
that while they live, they exist
within another sphere of splendor
they sleep, dream, taste fish, fruit,
they work, watch over their children.

Earth, you used to comfort me
when I was young and scolded
I'd gaze at the sea
and my heart would open up—
pour your balm once more
sustain me.
I want to think of love
as a story I heard once,
as if pain and absence
had only been described to me
and inside your font
I want to imagine our bodies

merging once more,
without pain
like larvae
loose in the world
losing in significance
gaining in love.

PERHAPS ALL PASSION IS COLDNESS

Perhaps all passion
is coldness,
I thought walking along the edge
of the precipice... silence,
and inside me even whiter,
steaming, milky;
words floating headless,
faces, meanings disintegrating,
all things falling and settling
down below.
Waves in the mist,
a whale I saw far away
spraying her watery song
to the ocean above,
and the ravine, green, overgrown
her muzzle only
resting on the sand,
the saint I never believed in
whose bells I heard and was comforted somehow—
darkness
ripped apart.

Passion seems to come
from the alchemy of ice,
a cold that keeps
pain unshared
and the core of grace
so deeply buried.
It lurks behind things,
like a bone,
an inflexible nerve, hard
incapable of fire,
something like an animal-doorkeeper
with one eye only
staring at chaos
motionless,
with only one ear
listening to silence.

JEALOUSY

Sundays he goes with that woman
and together they enjoy the desolate
countryside.
There they are, passing by the farms;
two dead pigs next to the fence,
their hooves stretched out in the afternoon;
light frost covers the mud,
the snow's gone,
but the earth's still silent
and alone.
Is it peace, is it torment
their love?
Lemon colored sun.
Who is she
what face
what breast?
The country is slowly packed with night,
there is nothing exotic
about this landscape; with what
passion he holds the woman;
like one body they glide into the room,
he takes off his shirt
his careworn sternum
smells sour sweat and fresh air,
slowly the bare branches recede
into memory
and the landscape renews itself inside them
in full spring.

THE FACE OF THE LOVER

The face of the lover
has no precise form,
and only touch can illuminate
its core.

The lover is secretive,
his acts make him muter still.
Only when forgotten by the world,
and he sits for hours
before the empty plate—
the gravey wiped clean—
something moves inside him
something begins to flow,
now he calls it memory
now he calls it fear.
Deeper still,
the plot of seedlings,
the sower always remains unknown.

She
always dwells on the erotic,
he alone enters
in its depths.
His body is born again
inside her and all around
her breasts,
he no longer shunts his dreams,
he's moist and turns gentle,
hard, and he suffers.
To others he gives account
to her he explains.
With closed, scented mouth,
with eyes freed in the dark,
the promise of himself
blazes again.
Crowned with his body's glow,

liberated,
he rises to the Seven Heavens.
He's just,
unburdened, childless—
he becomes the Adored.

If as they say love
is blind
it is because this
tiny light
concealed in the face of the trapped lover
blinds.

THE LOVERS' TIME

For lovers time's different—
elusive
without resolution the moments end,
the future's conjured out of the most splendid
themes of yesterday's love
parting is considered death—
and when passion ends
time no longer knows itself.

By the time I answer the grocer
we have said the first hello
and the dialogue with you
has began again
Bliss—the first sign of recognition,
lighthearted I leave with the shopping bag
if you've managed to touch me,
stooped, if the terrible look
of parting has returned.

I void, always void
the moment from the now
and I enter another time
dense and indivisible.

OUR LOVE HAD A COSMIC POWER

Our love had a cosmic
bewitching power
when slowly we'd stroll
swaying as if in a rowboat—
festival we were and song.
Dishevelled
with lint from the blankets
still on our neck
our voice
like the pleasures of the jackal and the thrush
caught in the wind.
We knew the answers
when the angels asked us at the door—
those guards who keep
the earthly sorrow
strictly apart from the divine.
(Yes here we will stay... —as long as it lasts...
—we wonder at the fox... how she runs...
—we'll write poems until deep old age
until the body's great pain comes...)

You never embrace
you never fear
death so much
as when in your hands
love
becomes a scepter
of cosmic power.

KATERINA ANGHELAKI-ROOKE

THE SUITORS

From my window
the garden seems to belong
elsewhere
and the house to travel
on a leaf.
Through the shutters
the sliced suitors
of my silence
conspire
disposing my life
like an after-dinner-drink
and the smell of the roast meat
from the feasting
of my endless waiting
reaches the upper floors.
The suitors buzz around me
dizzy in the blaze of my dazzling loneliness.
I look down on them
from a room filled with Odysseus.
I must not talk again
of his exquisite voice
the measure of uniqueness
that made him timeless from the start,
but of a change
a bright thread inside me.
I reach the core of myself
by waiting.
How to describe the kernel
when it's no longer sheltered
when naked and
fearless
throbbing not panting
asserts the stability
of time in me?

A gravity flows out of me
and invades the world,
and if the process continues
death could be of value

I hear shouting from below.
I too used to have mud in my hair
lemon blossoms behind my ear
and I used to shout with passion
break loose, smash the bonds.
But the bonds reach deep—
an attitude,
a game the self plays
on itself.

Now only one opening
behind it my small
secret shadow—
my natural habitat.
Shut inside the house
as inside time,
I gaze at the trees
as I would at God—
outside time—
I begin to understand
my presence
here
with you, and without you.
My flesh waits for you
but in my mind I saw you come
and leave again
long ago.

Faces exist in us alone
their eyes sailing
in our body's fluids.

THE LAST LIGHT

Where I plunged to find you
nothing exists anymore
and mute is the oracle of my heart.
You are an absolute form
inaccessible even by life.
You are a white speck
a drop of hazy water.
I want to destroy
my last light
as far as the eye can see,
not even a swallow I want on my horizon
not a single illusion.
My heart will be dead
but I——living still
will peer into nature
and I will call you summer.
Finally without memory
I will call you flower, until
legend lowers the curtain behind me,
facing me——a white wall
everything final and white
and I, a crushed cockroach.

Eleni Fourtouni

Eleni Fourtouni was born in 1933, in Vassara, a village in the mountains of Sparta. In 1953 she came to the United States as an exchange student. She studied Social Studies at Nasson College in Springvale, Maine, and Criminology at the University of New Haven. Soon after graduation she married a fellow student and devoted the next 16 years of her life to raising her son and daughter.

Fourtouni is the editor and translator of *Greek Women Poets:* a collection of poems by contemporary Greek poets, including her own work, and the author of *Monovasia*, a collection of love poems. *Greek Women in Concentration Camps*, journals, poems, and drawings by exiled women, edited and translated by Fourtouni, will be published this fall.

Fourtouni lives with her daughter Rachel and her son Russell in New Haven, but, like all Greek immigrants who are constantly possessed by the Homeric *nostos*, she spends much of her life flying between her two homelands.

Eleni Fourtouni

From MONOVASSIA

CHANSON D' AMOUR

1.

After seven months of famine
you offer your body
to my pleasure
first I choose
your tongue
firm and moist
on the swelling lips
my arid womb
floods with the warm fluids
your tender
persistent sucking
releases in my vitals
you suck the acid of your absence
out
you spread over my garden
dark
fertile soil
you plant a vine arbor
you tend the sapling well
until it flowers
and gives fruit
until the fruit—
large
ripe
succulent—
comes open
inside your mouth.

2.

Again
you are here
it is your head on the pillow
your hair just as I remember it
tangled raw silk
like the unbeliever
I touch
your lashes stroke my breasts
inundating me with light
I kiss the pulse
on your throat
I roll in your meadow
I drink in your fountain
I am delivered
from my cumbersome
multidimensionality
stripped of all surfaces
I am intact
elemental
I see you
I smell you
I taste you
you become my heartbeat.

3.

When my sleeping womb
stirs
moved by a memory
when it wakes
in this bed
where you have never slept
when it opens up
when it demands
your glowing sex
when you guide my hand
to the threshold of my cunt
when you want
the pleasure of watching me
caress my own body
I part open the outer lips
I expose the center
to your eyes
I stroke
the slowly emerging
kernel
I reach deep
and deeper still
I taste the pearls
of your salty tender sap
I dissolve
in the many springs
within
I spin a bridge
I float
I come
I bury myself
inside you.

4.

I am lifted
seven flights
up an attic room
in Paris
out of the keyhole
light flows
into the dark passage
you unlock the door
and let me in
rows of roses
climb the slanted walls
downy cushions
under our bare feet
on the borrowed bed
our quilt
waits
for new colors
new designs
you purify
you cool your hands
before they touch me
you string me through
in silk warp
weaving me
again and again
with threads of gold
threads of silver.

5.

Cancel
unreasonable journey
stop
unreasonable love

I ask you
do you argue
with the sun
do you demand
that the rain justify
her existence
do you question
the vastness of the sea

I tell you
love is reason enough
simple enough
it flows like a stream
like Ariadne's thread

I dare you
to cancel the wind.

6.

In Mani
there is no soil
only stones
no room for trees
and flowerbeds
but the seed
dropping
where the dark rock divides
will take root
will grow down
down
into the earth's center
will draw
from the light
from the fire
from the blood stored there
drop
by drop
it will draw for color
it will draw for fragrance
it will endure the drought
it will dare to shoot
a fragile stalk
up through
the grey vein of the granite
out into the glowing dawn
a scarlet flower
will unfold her petals
briefly
she will bask in blue
gathering the moment's offering
inside the shelter of her memory
slowly remaking the seed
for next year's flower.

Eleni Fourtouni

From POEMS TO LUCIFER

THE ARGUMENT

But I must
touch
not because
I don't believe
when you tell me
Now
and puffs
of irridescent silk
fill my body
or when you say
Here
and I can feel
the cyclamens
pushing
through the soil
I can see
the delicate
pink petals
unfolding
before even
the sun
can see them
I must touch
not because I doubt
I become the shore
that opens up
in 1000
tiny lips
popping gently
each time your breath
washes over me
and you say
Do it

I am not afraid to walk
on water
when you say
Come
I always come
when you summon me
over
and over
not knowing
how
I would enter
time again
live
in this world
again
from the beginning
I believed in you
I believed
in you
when you said
And you shall have a new body
and I drifted
on that ocean
until 99
waves lifted me
and brought me
down again

But I must touch you
now
not because I don't believe
in the miracle
of your word
I must touch you
because I lust for your body—
your body.

Halandri / Sept./1979

KLITA'S RING

1.

The inscription on the ring, a silver,
moonshaped disk, reads: ΚΛΕΙΤΑΔΩΡΟΝ
gift to Klita. A museum copy,
the original found in a woman's grave
unearthed on an island
in the Aegean Sea. No one knows
who, what that woman was. And we know
nothing about the giver of the ring.

But through his gift we can imagine something
of her life. Imagine him, on a morning of
a summer night when the moon was a silver
disk over the dark sea, stopping
at a silversmith's shop choosing
his telling gift, and on it
tracing her name——Klita. A name
lost. She must have died young, leaving
no daughters to bring her name to us.
Nothing but his gift survives of what
she must have been——a woman with slender hands;
a life marked by the phases
of the moon. The cast of her face,
the tone of her voice, unknown.

The moon, the ring, the name, and nothing more.

2.

When I finished what I knew of this
story, carefully enunciating the Greek
for you, a poem I meant to write
once about another moonshaped
ring, and a man from Flanders, the giver

of that ring, came to mind—
leaning on the stone wall, sharing
a cigarette, our bare backs pressed
against the salt-corroded
stones, I remembered the topaz, perfectly
round, perfectly luminous, set
in intricate silver filigree—on the sand,
within our arms' reach, a carafe
of ouzo and ice water, a single
glass we'd lift to an oversized plum-
of-a-sun rolling down the mountainrim,
to whitecapped breakers soon to be washed
in lavender and rose hues, to the night
waiting for us, and to the silvering moon,
full over the Aegean Sea—

It must have been the memory of
the full moon over another sea
the Flemish silversmith crafted in the shape
of that ring—the moon
the instant she slips behind cloudbanks,
the silver clouds clustering around her.

Leaning on the stone wall, sharing
a cigarette with you, I told you of that
ring, and of the man who on a summer
morning stopped at a silversmith's shop
and chose that moonshaped stone—
his last gift to me.

3.

Later that night, lying on thin
mattresses on the roof of our house, you said
astronomers predict one day the moon
will fall, will strike the earth, the earth

ELENI FOURTOUNI

will shake, will turn, will spin out of
course, the survivors, if any, will look—
you said—at empty skies forever. I remembered
then a dream I had—a telling dream—
predicting the end of love, the loss
of a beloved man: my ring had cracked,
a dreadful dark where once
the glowing stone had been.

The earth will shake, will turn, will spin...

It may well be. But that night
lying within your arms' reach,
I knew that the survivors, if any, will not
look at empty skies for long—
I knew that love will seek and find
another source of light.

AUBADE

The sun every morning
gliding through vines
through shutter slats
settling on our eyelids
days shimmering with cicadas
unrelenting sunlight
your body gleaming beside me
on my palm the smell of olive oil
I rubbed into your skin
you quiver as my tongue slides along your spine
my belly, my thighs
a nest around your hips

it's morning now
I sit under the same vines
ten days have passed since then
ten days filled with absence
I can almost see you on the east veranda—
the orange trees bend their branches toward you
the cat, away for a while from her demanding litter
purrs in the shade
the grapes glow overhead

(I smell your first cigarette
when you reach for the second
I get up
boil water for our coffee
cut the Zakynthino melon
spread wild cherry jam and thyme honey
on fresh bread

we lift each moment
carefully from the day's silver tray)

And that's how it was for 22 mornings

Eleni Fourtouni

on the 23rd morning
you reach out to me
saying nothing
and I get up in silence
in silence I bring our breakfast—
the pot of coffee
the Zakynthino melon
the bread with wild cherry jam and thyme honey—
I set them beside the mattress
on the marble floor
in the cool white room

the gauze curtains billow in the breeze
the eucalyptus trees
bordering the street outside our house
always still until now
always listening in silence
toss and turn and sway

pleading with you to stay.

THE PICK

I think of that day in May
when we sat on the cliffs of the Atlantic coast
strangers still
speaking in metaphor

I remember your words now—
in another coast
another season—
now that you've gone from this island
where we watched white ships
glide in the harbor
and glide out again
gone from this garden—golden
with oranges—where the abandoned kittens
cried, gone from this white-curtained room
where unrelenting sunlight
glided through shutter slats
waking us to the multitude of mornings
of our numbered days

the cliffs were eroded, covered with gaps
in the shape of dissolved clam
and mussel shells
fossils of seaweed, pieces of coral

there is beauty in loss—you said
touching the eroded rock

I remember this now
in this winter garden
now that your absence digs inside my belly
like that pick you dug the hole
to bury the last of the summer kittens—
under the orange trees
where their mother cries
and mates again.

VALENTINE

Come my lover
the larks nest again in the palm tree
and flocks of seagulls hover
over the frothy trails
of ferryboats

all is ready by now my lover
the wine has blended with resin long
enough, branches of almond tree
bloom in each white room
sunlight streams
through the shutters and lies
on your side of the bed

today I'll paint my toenails red
rinse with henna my hair

Come now my lover.

EXPELLED

1.

You enter through my temples.
My skull gave way to your gaze
as a spiderweb would to your breath.
Your law carved on granite crushed
my eyeballs. I could see like Teiresias then
but my vision was Cassandra's vision.

I saw you waiting like an intransigent God—
a willful, a harsh taskmaster—
watching for my transgressions
amending nothing, forgetting nothing
remembering nothing.

Your will, an immense icicle
suspended over my breasts.

Your will, immune to spring thaw.

2.

I wanted my scream to be knives, butcher hooks
shards of glass. I wanted my scream to be fire.

But you are invulnerable, untouchable.
You are the eagle that rips me up.
You claw at my intestines. Your beak pulls
and tears. Your beak devours.

What God, what Demon sends you?

What is the crime, the sin, the service?

3.

You fired the coup-de-grâce, threw the pistol
over the pier and carried my body to the house.
You placed me on the bed, you lit the candles,
poured the wine. Your naked body cast a giant shadow—
a cyclops looming over me, an enormous fish
throbbing between his thighs.

Your hands cup my breasts, your tongue
like a flame in my mouth
your teeth bleed my lips.

Do it you said
Now you said
Come you said. Your cunt is a storm you said
your cunt is wild it bites and lashes
and kisses you said.

We neglected nothing, forgot nothing
performed every ritual, one by one, over
and over, until the sun reached the top of
the cypress tree, until the day shimmered with
cicadas.

Go you said. *Do it* you said. *Now* you said.

4.

My room is like a funeral parlor
vases and clay jars filled with red
carnations and gladiolas—my daughter's
offerings. She alone knows I've died.
She alone waited for the white boat,
signed the papers, paid for the passage.

When she comes in to tend the flowers, she steps
lightly, speaks to me in whispers, shoos the flies
from my lips.

We watch.

5.

At the pier you watch the ferryboats disappearing
behind the island, then the sun setting, the moon
silvering. As you flick your cigarette into the dark sea
the ring I gave you flashes me a signal.

Aegina/June 7/1981